G000054734

Hidden Riches of Secret Places

Hidden Riches of Secret Places

Isabel Henderson.

The Pentland Press Ltd.,
EDINBURGH CAMBRIDGE DURHAM

Other books by the author:
Contemplative Meditation: A Deeper Approach to
Life and Worship.

© Isabel Henderson 1991
First published in 1991 by
The Pentland Press Ltd
Brockerscliffe
Witton le Wear
Durham
All rights reserved
Unauthorised duplication contravenes applicable laws

ISBN 1 872795 04 8

Typeset by Print Origination (NW) Ltd., Formby, Liverpool L37 8EG
Printed and bound by Antony Rowe Ltd., Chippenham

Jacket design by Geoff Hobbs

Foreword

When someone we are fond of makes us a present of a little jewel case we are naturally very happy and excited, never doubting that it contains something which will be very precious to us. Only when we try to open the case, do we realise that we need to use the key to see fully what we hold in our hands. That is what the Bible is like for many of us.

We own it, we believe in it, but do we try to use the key which enables us to understand more perfectly the hidden treasures in its pages?

Acknowledgement

Without the help and encouragement given to me by Marian V Dunlop, the founder of The Fellowship of Meditation, I doubt if this book would ever have gone into print. I feel sure, therefore, that my gratitude can best be expressed by a readiness to continue in this work and to help in whatever way I can to further the teaching of Contemplative Meditation in the widest sense.

Those of you who wish to know more about this way of meditation, or to continue exploring the life-giving possibilities which its practice can offer us through finding oneness with God should contact

Fellowship of Meditation
6 Prince of Wales Road
Dorchester
Dorset
DT1 1PW

where many books by Marian V Dunlop can be obtained.

Contents

Introduction......viii

PART ONE

The Hidden Inner Meaning......1

PART TWO

Silence Yields the Key......7

PART THREE

Stillness Opens the Door. Meditations for Everyday Use.

"Be Still, take hold of my strength and be at peace with me."......13

"Behold, I have loved thee with an everlasting Love and long to give thee Life"......17

"I will be still and know the deep and luminous calm of union with Thee."......21

"I am come to lead thee into the light of life."......25

"Trust thou only in me and I will give thee the power of Righteousness."......28

"I am Infinite Peace within thee. With my peace I give thee rest."......32

"I am Infinite Love within thee. I will give thee the hidden riches of secret places."......36

"Eternal Love within me. Thee only will I serve."......40

"Oh God, give me Knowledge, Knowledge of thy Health and Healing Power within me."......44

"I am Eternal Life within thee. Behold, I make all things new."......48

"My servant art thou, in whom I shall break into glory."...52

Thanksgiving......56

Words of Life......57

Index......58

Introduction

This book attempts to lead us towards a way of contemplation which is a deeper form of prayer and inner communion with God, who is the source of life within us.

No one can teach us Contemplative Meditation unless we are first drawn to it by an inner longing of the soul for God, which only God can satisfy, but we can be greatly helped by a method of practice which if we use it faithfully can make us ready for and receptive to, all that God seeks to reveal to us.

A sentence is used to focus our attention upon God. This sentence may express what God himself would say to us, or our own prayerful response to His call and teaching.

We gently hold our chosen sentence in the mind, turning all other thoughts away; we do not wish to stimulate the mental activity about the sentence but rather let it help the mind to become still.

Only when the conscious mind rests from its ceaseless thinking about its own affairs and the personal self is silent, can we distinguish the still small voice of the spirit from the clamour of the world. Our attention is thus focussed upon our meditation. The divine essence which it contains sinks down through the conscious mind into the unconscious nature which is the source of so much of our distress, bringing peace and regeneration to the whole of our being.

The contemplation of God is the ultimate aim of this way of meditation and should this little excursion into its beginnings appeal to us, we are free to venture further at our own pace into new areas of spiritual experience in the company of God.

If, when we first read through this book we feel drawn to the practice of Contemplative Meditation, we should return to this passage afterwards by following the basic instructions for the proper use of our sentence. We should work our way more slowly and in greater detail through the following pages. Only by patient practice can we develop in the way God wills for each individual and gain our own spiritual experience. For God can reveal to us His truth only when we learn to be still and listen to Him within our own soul.

PART ONE

The Hidden Inner Meaning

The Hidden Inner Meaning

Everything in life has both a hidden inner meaning and an outer visible form; nothing is exactly as it appears to us. Even we as individuals, have a secret inner life, as well as an outer visible appearance and personality which can be recognised.

The Bible too has an inner hidden meaning as well as the outer form which we know and love, and when we open its pages there is much which conveys a double message.

It all depends on our approach to the Bible and our particular sensitivity to the words, what message it reveals to us. Some people treat the Bible simply as history which can be proved by other means; other people take the words of scripture quite literally. Yet both the Old Testament and the New are more than an historical record or a literal guide to life. For although the Bible has both these qualities it contains much more besides: it contains Eternal Truth.

In the Old Testament, for instance, the commandment tells us 'Thou shalt not commit adultery' Exod. 20:14. The outer meaning is quite obvious but the deeper meaning is that we must not even think it in our hearts.

In turning to the New Testament, all Jesus's teaching contains an inner hidden meaning. Jesus taught the people by parable; word pictures of daily life with a meaning which they had to look for and remember. Why did Jesus teach in parables? Because it was the story which would stick in their minds. In time the deeper spiritual meaning would emerge as experience quickened their understanding, for those who wanted to hear and act upon His teaching would be able to identify themselves with the stories and learn to live more and more in his likeness. Can we appreciate just why Jesus gave spiritual teaching in this obscure way? Why he did not explain what He meant more plainly? The people were simply not ready to receive it.

1

Let us remember that the people to whom Jesus mostly spoke were Jews. From birth they had been taught to live literally by the letter of the law. They were not expected to think for themselves but Jesus gave a new responsibility towards life which at first they found difficult to accept, therefore an indirect approach was made through familiar scenes and objects to which they could easily relate.

We know how young people cannot be taught about life directly because their understanding is limited; they have to learn through experience as they grow: so it is with spiritual teaching even today.

As we are able to be entrusted with new truths further enlightenment is given. We grow spiritually and our understanding increases. It would be useless therefore to give the deeper truths of the scriptures to those who were not already familiar with their outward meaning and accepted it. That is what the parables are all about. If the outer meaning satisfies, the rest would be wasted on us.

If on the other hand the recognisable story strikes an inner cord of understanding in our hearts a link is formed between us and the ever living Christ, enabling us to find the key to the inner kingdom of the Spirit which is within our own soul.

Let us take up our Bible now, realising that the words it contains are but the vehicle by which eternal truths are first conveyed to our hearts and minds, but that we need time to let these words sink in and expand into truth and life within us. For the Bible speaks to each one of us in different ways, because we are all individual in the sight of God. As our Lord's words come alive for us, they speak personally to each individual soul.

We need only take time to inwardly digest what we read till its spiritual meaning can be made known to us.

Let us turn to the New Testament, to the parable of the sower scattering his seed, in both fertile and infertile soil alike. This is a perfect example of Jesus's teaching and could be received or rejected by those who heard him.

This is the parable which Jesus had to explain even to His disciples. Luke 8: 5-15. "A sower went out to sow his seed

2

and as he sowed some fell by the wayside and it was trodden down and the fowls of the air devoured it. And some fell upon rock and as soon as it was sprung up it withered away because it lacked moisture. And some fell among thorns and the thorns sprung up with it and choked it. And other fell on good ground and sprang up and bare fruit a hundredfold. And when He had said these things he cried, 'He that hath ears to hear let him hear.' And His disciples asked him saying 'What might this parable be?' And he said 'Unto you it is given to know the mystery of the Kingdom of God but to others in parables, that seeing they might not see and hearing they might not understand.

"'Now the parable is this: The seed is the word of God, Those by the wayside are they that hear; then cometh the devil and taketh away the word out of their hearts, lest they should believe and be saved.

"'They on the rock are they which when they hear, receive the word with joy: and these have no root, so for a time believe, and in time of temptation fall away. And that which fell among thorns are they which when they have heard, go forth and, choked with cares and riches and pleasures of this life, bring no fruit to perfection.

"'But that on the good ground are they, which in an honest and good heart having heard the word, keep it and bring forth fruit with patience.'"

Jesus's teaching is very much alive to-day. His Spirit teaches us from within when we turn to Him and listen to Him in the silence, of our own hearts and minds.

Our lives are like parables. They each have a deeper meaning and purpose. It is only when we truly seek to follow that purpose we can hope to understand even a little of its meaning. For Jesus said, "The Kingdom of God is within you and who-so-ever shall know himself shall find it." Luke 17:21.

St. Paul said, "Know ye not that ye are the temple of God and the Spirit of God dwelleth in you." 1.Cor. 3:16.

Our lives might be measured against the parable of the seed in the fertile ground for we hold the seed of the Spirit deep within the soil of our being and in the silence we may tend and increase its growth into fruitfulness.

3

PART TWO

Silence Yields the Key

Silence Yields the Key.

Contemplative Meditation is not a new form of prayer. It has been practised since ancient times but it has been adapted to suit the needs of a changing Western culture which has somewhere lost its direct contact with the indwelling Spirit. We need to re-establish that inner communion with God and find a discipline and method to help us.

Silence is the key which helps us most in the first instance. Yet so many people shy away and are really afraid of it. Is that because of what silence may reveal about ourselves? Or perhaps we are afraid of the still small voice of the conscience which is the beginning of enlightenment if we will but heed its prompting.

Let us take courage and trust the silence of meditation, for by the protection of the word of Christ, we come to know ourselves, and by the guidance of the indwelling Spirit seek the Kingdom of God which is within us.

In the meditations which follow many aspects of daily life may be touched upon for both the teaching and practice of Contemplative Meditation become a way of life. Should we find ourselves identifying with any of the situations mentioned in the following, we may be already sensitive to the inner promptings of the Spirit and would do well to follow the practice as described earlier and find the hidden riches that await our own discovery. For Christ it is that brings the human and the divine within us into one harmonious whole in His name.

As we read the passages for meditation we may feel the need to pause and consider some points. This should be done before we attempt to meditate. Do not take a busy mind into the silence making it very difficult to find real stillness and openness to the Spirit's teaching.

In order to derive most benefit from the following meditations each sentence should be used at the most suitable time for each one of us, daily, for five to six minutes at a time. Gradually we can lengthen this time as the practice becomes easier to us. Each sentence enfolds some aspect of the divine nature of Christ. This helps us grow in awareness of His presence.

Let us take up the key of Spiritual Truth in our hearts. Let us open the inner door of the secret place of the most High within our own souls, and in stillness the Spirit can bring us a little nearer to His perfection.

This form of meditation, although it asks for both dedication and trust, does not make great demands upon our physical or mental abilities. This practice can help us recapture the lost capacity for inner attunement to God, which has been so long neglected by this materially minded world that we seem to have lost our sense of direction. Yet by quiet acceptance of this practice, it can become a natural way of finding inner communion with God by which we grow in knowledge of Him.

No discipline is ever easy, especially in the early stages, but it is helpful at first if we make sure that we sit in an upright but comfortable position, in which the freeflow of breath, and the circulation of the blood are un-hampered by any tightness. For the very air which we breathe, not only bears purifying oxygen to the body, but also carries with it The Breath of Life,—The Breath of The Spirit, to all who are ready to acknowledge and draw upon it. By this means the body too can receive new strength and vitality, both from without and within.

In this restful, receptive attitude, we leave behind the problems of the moment to seek renewal and inner enlightenment from the Spirit of Christ. We use a divinely inspired sentence to focus our unruly minds upon the Light of Christ indwelling us, for it is His Spirit behind the words which enlightens us when we of ourselves are still. It is the dedication of each one of us to this end that contributes to the real success of our practice throughout the months and years. May it lead us into closer communion with Christ, who is The Light of Life.

One of the most important points to note is the difference between discursive and contemplative meditation. In the discursive form our minds are encouraged to analyse and ponder a situation; to reach our own conclusions. In contemplative meditation we learn to still the mind from consecutive thinking. This does not mean by-passing the conscious mind, leaving it empty and a prey to other influences, but it does mean keeping the mind alert, attentive to the words of our meditation, and while turning towards the power of Christ's love, His Spirit will illumine the words for us and we grow in knowledge of Him.

Many of our sentences ask us to be still but the very familiarity of the words tempts us to slide past them to seek something more exciting. If we can master the art of stillness it can, in time, lead us towards contemplation of the Almighty.

We can be still in body if we really wish, but stilling the mind is a different matter. An athlete learns to control the body through discipline, concentration and practice; he wishes to become master of his own body. Contemplative Meditation has to be approached with the same kind of dedication, if we mean to be master of our own mind.

Constancy in practice and the will to succeed towards our goal of communion with the indwelling spirit will surely be rewarded and we gain much in the process through a deeper understanding of ourselves. For example, when we come to our time of silence we begin to realise just how much our minds rule over us; we need to take steps to become masters in our own house. The senses offer so many attractions that the mind can scarcely resist attending to them, till we learn to deal patiently and quietly with each of these hindrances, turning them away one by one till they no longer trouble us.

Some of the more subtle blocks to stilling the mind are hidden below the surface of consciousness and we find help in letting them be released.

One example of this, might be, in the way in which we present a bright pleasant image and personality to the world, yet how much does that image differ from the thoughts and feelings which we keep to ourselves, our failures, our weaknesses? It can sometimes be the discord between these two sides of our nature that makes stilling the mind more difficult. If we can hold to the truth of our meditation in silence, letting the negative past, our disappointments, our hurts slip away from us, even for an instant, we can reach a deeper stillness where there will be no jarring notes of disharmony in our consciousness. We will be single-minded towards the spirit of Love indwelling us and His power can heal and strengthen us. When we co-operate with the healing power of Christ in this way, His spirit ever draws us to himself, so that our lives can come a little nearer to His perfection. This way of meditation can lead to a more intimate and personal relationship with Christ because it affects each of us, according to our receptivity and our need. Each sentence we use is like a key which opens that area of our consciousness to which it directly appeals, awakening our individual response to it. This helps the spirit behind our meditation to work within that area of our receptivity, preparing us for that deeper communion with Christ which we seek.

The process of healing we embark upon is carried out, not only by the spirit behind our meditation reaching *in* through our consciousness but, by the same Spirit of Christ reaching *out* through our stillness. When we come through a meditation such as this, all that hinders the deeper approach to our Lord is melted away by His forgiving love. Or in His wisdom our Lord may reveal to the conscious mind those things which we need to know, and work through, under His loving care.

As we go within, we are protected by the divine influence of our sentence, till by degrees we reach that stillness to which our Lord calls us. As we rest there in safety and in trust, the power of His love is free within us. We are one with Him and His spirit reaches out into the whole of our being to heal and strengthen us.

We trust ourselves to the healing power of love ever working within us.

10

PART THREE

Stillness Opens the Door

Stillness Opens the Door.

Meditations for everyday use.

"Be Still, take hold of My Strength and be at Peace with Me"

If any of us are new to this practice and are really interested in Contemplative Meditation, we have possibly been reading and talking to others about the subject. Reading and talking about the practice is one thing, but gaining experience of it is quite another. In this way of meditation our aim is to deepen our awareness of Christ as ever present with us, to let the light of his peace be brought to bear on all that we feel, think and do.

We focus our inner attention in this meditation upon two aspects of the divine nature of Christ, so that we might absorb something of His strength and peace, into our lives. Let us look at our sentence again.

"Be Still, take hold of My Strength and be at Peace with Me"

Notice this word 'Peace'–it is an example of what are known as 'Words of Life'; that is to say, aspects of the Divine Nature of God. Further examples are listed at the end of this booklet. Sentences normally use one or more such 'Words of Life.'

We should have no difficulty in accepting this sentence as a divine statement for it embodies the essence of much of Christ's teaching. Direct quotes from scripture are not always used. Frequently quoted passages can become so familiar that they lose their impact upon us, therefore the feeling behind the words escapes us. A condensed passage, from Biblical teaching, which we can hold in our minds, might have quite a new ring of spiritual truth when its essence touches the heart and stirs our desire for further enlightenment and understanding.

When we listen to the words of our meditation we are accepting Christ's teaching, as given 2000 years ago. That, does not belong only to the written word, it is given by the living Spirit of Christ, even now, and we receive it in the silence of our own hearts and minds.

To be still is our first step, and to realise that it is the bustling self-assertive activity of our own minds that so often prevents us seeing our Lord at the centre of our lives, when we come to our times of silence. We cannot receive the whole truth of our meditation while our consciousness is disturbed on the surface by our prevailing moods, our busyness, our worries. We gladly take the opportunity to withdraw to a quiet place for a while till our whole consciousness becomes placid, reflecting the words. Only then, can the truth of our sentence reach the depth of our innermost being and the Spirit of peace make Himself known to us.

"Be still, take hold of My Strength and be at Peace with Me"

Pause for silent meditation.

"Take hold of My Strength".

These words almost seem like a contradiction to being still, for strength, to our minds often suggest some form of activity—doing something. But this sentence asks us first to *be*, then to *do*. For, in the silence of our meditation the intellect stands still, learning to function in a new and vital way, being like a lens, through which the words can shine, till their spiritual content reaches the soul and their power is magnified by His Spirit indwelling us. Then we take hold of Divine Strength and let it quietly flow into our whole being.

We can often misdirect or even misuse our human energies but Divine Strength cannot be received if we are out of tune with the Spirit of Christ. We need to recognise and pay attention to the still small voice of the Spirit within us and wait patiently upon Him in silence.

During each time of meditation we can actually be living, for however brief a moment, in the kingdom of God which is within us. For, as we open our hearts and minds to Christ, acknowledging our need of Him, He answers our call. The spiritual power of our sentence comes alive in us and we make it our own. Then we go out from our meditation knowing that what we have received in stillness will influence our work, our decisions, our relationships with others, day by day.

There is surely no greater source of peace, than in the knowledge that we can return again and again, to be renewed in strength in the silence of our own hearts and minds. As we grow spiritually we find that, even during our most active moments, we carry within us that still centre of God's peace which we learn to draw upon ever more deeply, no matter the turmoil around us.

"Be still, take hold of My Strength and be at Peace with Me"

Pause for silent meditation.

This sentence can become a favourite with many of us because it speaks so directly to our need. Owing to our initial difficulty in becoming really still it takes a little time before the results of our practice can be felt in our lives. Yet the fruits of silence will come forth into our consciousness when the Spirit of our meditation leads our hearts and minds toward true contemplation.

In this way of Meditation there is a certain amount of teaching, but it is always balanced by practice. The real power of our meditation comes through the living silence, when the mind is alert and receptive to the truth. What any speaker says only prepares us for the silence and we must resist the temptation to commit to memory what has been said, for, by keeping the mind active in that way, we hinder the entrance of spiritual truth to the deeper areas where the

15

greater work needs to be done. Our aim is to receive and inwardly digest what we have heard at a deeper level of our nature, for the conscious mind is only a part of the whole being. There is the unconscious, which plays a greater part in our health and well being than we realise. And, while the conscious mind is listening, the unconscious is also open and receptive to the words.

As we learn to become still, in the truth for which our sentence stands, there is a harmonising of the conscious and unconscious natures and we find peace within ourselves. We are in tune with the indwelling Spirit of Christ and know that strength and peace that the world cannot give.

"Be still, take hold of My Strength and be at Peace with Me".

Pause for silent meditation.

"Behold, I have loved thee with an everlasting Love and long to give thee Life."

By using this form of sentence we are constantly called to the right attitude of alert awareness and expectancy, for the word "Behold", often used by our Lord to arrest people's attention, should also stop us in our mental tracks and help us concentrate upon the truth which follows.

"I have loved thee with an everlasting Love and long to give thee Life."

The patient longing expressed in this sentence only emphasises our inability to feel and know God's kind of love in our hearts, for our ideas of love are often so limited, and we keep them tucked away in separate compartments of life. We think in terms of a mother's love, love of sweethearts, love of friends, love of country, love of God.

All these forms of love spring from human emotions and personality which colours their expression through us, each but an imperfect reflection of Divine Love.

God's love is all embracing and profound. It is given without limit or condition. The infinite power of God's love is stronger than the pull of any human emotion or personality. It is everlasting and divine. If only we will turn to God and let our feeble expressions of love be purified, strengthened and guided by Him, we would grow in His likeness.

We have become so used to living according to our own familiar ways that we leave little room to experience that deeper form of love which, if we are honest, we are a little afraid of, because it can so often lead to sacrifice or suffering, of one kind or another.

Yet a life which is denied the true depths of love or

17

suffering is also incapable of experiencing their fruits. It is a barren existence in which the seeds of true love waiting within can become sterile from finding no season of fruitfulness and sharing.

We recognise the outward signs of God's love in the world about us. We need to become more and more aware of the Spirit of His love seeking expression through us. We have to develop an awareness of the everlasting nature of the love of God by being still in His presence, in order to let its all embracing influence be felt in our hearts.

The poet had the right idea when he questioned the value of a life so full of care that left no time to stand and stare. The writer knew the necessity of pausing to drink in the detail of his surroundings, before it could be reproduced through the medium of words.

In contemplative meditation we go much deeper than to observe the visible, for not only do we recognise the outward sign of God's Love in the world, we acknowledge our need to become more and more aware of the Spirit of His Love, seeking expression within our own lives. To help satisfy this inner need we practise disciplining ourselves by disregarding our physical surroundings. We ignore the distractions of the outward senses and give our whole attention to the Spirit of Love within us.

As we rightly use our sentence as a focus for our minds, we are enabled to let go some of the things which hinder our spiritual progress; for the power of eternal love will lessen their weight upon us, and when the mind is still and one pointed towards God, we are filled by the inflowing of His more abundant Life, as we open ourselves to receive It.

Let us respond to the call of God's love in the knowledge that His infinite patience is as everlasting as His love.

"Behold, I have loved thee with an everlasting Love and long to give thee Life."

Pause for silent meditation.

The meditation we are using can be found in a slightly

different form in Jeremiah: "Behold, I have loved thee with an everlasting love, therefore with loving kindness have I drawn thee." Jer. 31:3.

Jeremiah echoes the word of God in a way which might help us realise that when we cease ignoring God, in our independent self centred way, and let ourselves be drawn to Him, our whole being will be infused by His pure Spirit of loving kindness. Through the tender mercies of God the many varied situations in which we find ourselves can be seen from a new angle through the inner eye of love. Then all our human relationships will be lit by a new understanding and concern which previously we lacked. For, the Spirit of God's loving kindness when awakened within us, can also touch and awaken that same kind of love within the hearts of those with whom we come into contact, leading us all towards a whole new aspect of living.

We find the love of God beyond our comprehension only because our hearts and minds are not yet big enough to contain it. Therefore, our desire to express it, must not depend on our own limited conceptions of it.

Let us simply open ourselves with complete trust towards God and accept whole heartedly that which He offers, for when we are prepared to receive only that which fits in with our own ideas, we limit God in His greatest gift of all—the gift of newness of life itself.

As we hear the words of our meditation again in the stillness, let them make an everlasting impression upon us.

"Behold, I have loved thee with an everlasting Love and long to give thee Life."

Pause for silent meditation.

When we reach the last silence of our meditation, we should be experiencing some change in consciousness, for when our will and desire become one, in response to the word of God, we are irresistibly drawn to Him. When the heart and mind unite with the Spirit of love in stillness, the body too becomes quietly content awaiting the renewal of strength and vitality which we have grown to rely upon for daily living. For meditation does not induce a state of idleness as it allows the light of eternal love to direct us in all that we feel think and do. Every sentence we use brings to our inner attention, some aspect of the love of God, be it Infinite Peace, Divine Wisdom etc.

God's love is both their root and their flowering, for the seeds of that love have been planted deep within each one of us in readiness for that moment of inner sensitivity and awareness, which can effect its quickening.

Each time of silence is a time of inner enlightenment and awakening whether we realise it or not. We are engaged in a process of spiritual growth and learning, given at the pace at which we are able to make use of it, to enrich our whole existence. And, when we trust all to the Spirit of eternal love within, we begin to know the meaning of that newness of life, which our Lord spoke of when He said, "I am come that ye may have life and have it more abundantly". John 10:10.

Let us now, through the eternal love of Christ, receive and share the more abundant life which God so longs to give.

"Behold, I have loved thee with an everlasting Love and long to give thee Life."

Pause for silent meditation.

"I will be still and know the deep and luminous calm of union with Thee".

As we prepare to use this sentence for meditation, perhaps for the first time, we may find a little difficulty in responding to its profound and tranquil atmosphere, especially if we have had a trying day. To help us make this calm aproach to our times of silence, let us remember our Lord's words: "Peace, be still", Mark 4:39; for, when Jesus quietened the storm at sea, His disciples were far from being calm. Their hearts and minds were full of fear for their safety. Yet, when they heard their Master's words and knew the peace of His presence, they too became calm and trusting.

When we come to our times of silence, our whole consciousness may be likened to that lake. When the water was disturbed on the surface, it could not hold a perfect reflection; yet, when the wind had dropped and the lake became calm, even its hidden depths would become luminous with light. Our Lord knew and trusted the Spirit of God within Him so completely that He could have slept right through the storm, had not His disciples called to Him. We have to remind ourselves, that through all the storms of life, both within and without, Christ is in our ship with us, hearing our call. As we become calm in His presence, the light of His peace illumines our whole consciousness, calming our fears.

Let us hear our master's words now, in the silence, for they have lost nothing of their power, and let the peace of Christ Himself calm the storms on the surface of our consciousness till we are able to hold a more perfect reflection of His Light.

As our silence deepens we absorb something more of that deep and luminous calm throughout our whole being which brings us nearer to union with Christ Himself.

21

"I will be still and know the deep and luminous calm of union with Thee."

Pause for silent meditation.

There is more to our consciousness than the thoughts and feelings which engage our attention, for, as the mind becomes still and our sentence begins to work for us, its divine power reaches deeper into the unconscious nature where so much healing takes place.

The unconscious is a store house of past human experiences–be they destructive or helpful–which are mostly forgotten. Many of these may belong to early childhood, but some we have gathered from a mixture of differing beliefs and events which still influence the society in which we live. These collective experiences can show in our individual lives, instinctive reactions to habits of thought and feeling, helping to make us the kind of person we are.

Yet the unconscious is more than just a reservoir of past experience, for, when we become alive to the presence of the Spirit within us, His light will shine out through the unconscious mind banishing the shadows, bringing His peace and understanding to the whole of our consciousness.

The human soul has been likened to a lens through which the spirit can shine out into the whole mind to heal and strengthen. This lens is still in process of being cleansed and polished to meet its true purpose.

When the soul becomes more perfected and the unconscious is transparent enough to hold the divine light of peace in our hearts, we become a focus for Christ's light and peace in the world, for the body is an instrument of the soul and the soul is an instrument of the Spirit.

As we use our sentence to clear the shadows from the conscious mind we help the process of inner cleansing to proceed, for, when we truly seek union with Christ in stillness, His Spirit comes forth to our aid. The inner clouds of doubt, mistaken belief, are gently dissolved and a deep and luminous calm takes their place.

Shadows may sometimes return but they can never become

central to our consciousness while we seek union with the indwelling Christ in stillness.

"I will be still and know the deep and luminous calm of union with Thee".

Pause for silent meditation.

We can look at life in two ways and see two different pictures. We can look out and see the kind of life we are making for ourselves or we can look within and try to glimpse that picture which the Creator holds for us, a life lived in close harmony with the Holy Spirit of Christ, who holds all creation in His care.

As we go about our daily routine we most often fit into the first picture of life, for we feel ourselves to be completely independent beings, and this indeed, from the human angle, is true.

We have each been given free will and the right to make the best use of the opportunities which offer themselves within our own situation and environment. But we often forget that we should also fit into the second picture, one with Christ at all levels of living.

These two aspects of life may at first seem rather difficult to reconcile, yet, when we remember that we are not only of human origin but also of God begotten, we each therefore have a particular part to play within the divine plan, as well as our outward human independence.

We have a hidden inner life of dependence on God which we have to recognise before our spiritual needs can be satisfied and our true human birthright fulfilled.

When our aim is to seek union with Christ in stillness there will be no wasted energy scattered in unsuitable directions, for Christ's words will so illumine our hearts and minds that we are lead into the right areas of action which best suit our temperament and our spiritual growth. Our lives become full of joy and purpose, as we practise more and more to relate inwardly to Christ and outwardly to others.

These two aspects of our nature gradually blend into one harmonious whole and we find union with Christ becomes more possible.

"I will be still and know the deep and luminous calm of union with Thee".

Pause for silent meditation.

"I am come to lead thee into the Light of Life."

When we set out upon any journey we usually have a definite destination and purpose in mind, and, if we are unfamiliar with the way, we keep checking to make sure we travel in the right direction. This is surely the wisdom with which we should carry out any undertaking. Therefore we should never be so unwise as to journey in the spiritual way without constantly re-establishing our true aim and purpose, which is to seek communion with the indwelling Christ, and, by constantly consulting His inner guidance, to ensure that we travel in the right direction.

In conversation with others we gain confidence in learning about the many varied ways by which we were lead towards this way of meditation. Think then of the infinite peace and security which we can enjoy in faithful meditation upon Christ, when we listen to His words within and outwardly act upon them in our lives.

For our Lord said, "I am the way, the truth and the Life." John 14:6.

He that followeth me shall not walk in darkness but shall have the light of life." John 8:12.

Prof. Wm. Barclay wrote in one of his books, "Life with Christ is to be found by listening. No man can find any way unless he is prepared to listen to someone who knows the way. He who would find life with Christ must listen to the Lord of life, and the energy of action must proceed from the stillness of listening."

Our Lord said, "He that followeth me shall not walk in darkness but shall have the light of life."

May the words of our meditation so fill the stillness of our listening that we take with us something of the truth and life behind the words into all our living.

"I am come to lead thee into the Light of Life."

Pause for silent meditation.

This sentence as we read or hear it is simply the vehicle by which our Lord conveys His message to us. We hold the words gently in our minds till they keep all other thoughts away. They expand into truth and life itself, for the Spirit behind our meditation is free within us and the process of inner spiritual enlightenment is quickened.

This expansion of consciousness does not take place until our restless minds are slowed down and become still. For it is not our own ideas about the sentence that are of importance, it is what the Spirit reveals to us, when we of ourselves are still, not thinking but awaiting His inner enlightenment.

Therefore, by this way of meditation we are not only using a sentence to bring our restless minds and wills under control, we are learning that by turning the mind in towards the Spirit by the power of His words we are being freed from the grip of our own negative emotions. Thus, we are able to open that inner door of our souls, to find a much safer and more tranquil area of our being which we need to know and use.

This deep spiritual area is what our Lord called the Kingdom of God within us. Yet we keep this inner kingdom so closed up and hidden away, even though it is there that our Lord can most effectively work in and through us, fitting us for the fullness of Life which he offers.

Let the living words of this meditation come alive for us till the light of Christ's spirit within us opens that inner door of our soul, where all things are possible in His name.

"I am come to lead thee into the Light of Life."

Pause for silent meditation.

There are many kinds of darkness to be found, both in the world around us and also within ourselves. Physical darkness we know and sometimes even fear because of what it might conceal. Yet not all darkness is grim or menacing. It may simply be absence of light. We need the relief of night as an aid to sleep, refreshing us for the coming day.

Mental darkness takes many forms and shades. It may be due to ignorance, lack of knowledge of God, or even of ourselves. Much of this inner darkness we have absorbed through the general accumulation of wrong beliefs and habits of past generations, as well as that which we generate for ourselves by thoughtless acts of disobedience to God's law of Love. Yet, in our times of silence, our Lord can disperse these shadows, or teach us to understand and come to terms with our own personal darkness by the inpouring of His Light, when we let Him.

But there is yet another kind of darkness with which we are less familiar, but which we can come to know and love. For when we become really still in mind and body, we can find a rare, spiritual darkness which protects and heals. God uses this kind of darkness to shield us from the full radiance of His Spirit, till we are made ready to come into His nearer presence. For, as we come to know God in our hearts, we can recognise the activity of His Spirit, ceaselessly at work in the world. For example: because of Moses' obedience and devotion to God he was able to sense His Presence in the burning bush. Similarly, during the transfiguration of Christ, God concealed Himself within a cloud, yet the disciples recognised His presence and were amazed.

We learn to seek this healing darkness within us, and give thanks for its sheltering, living Peace.

Isaiah understood and accepted God's promise to him, "I will give thee the treasures of darkness, and the hidden riches of secret places." Isaiah 45:3.

We find the presence of God in the secret place of the Most High within. There the treasures of darkness are gained through each human shadow overcome, and the hidden riches are found as we are able to look upon them by the Light of Eternal Love.

"I am come to lead thee into the Light of Life."

Pause for silent meditation.

27

"Trust thou only in Me and I will give thee the power of Righteousness."

"Trust thou only in Me."

This is one of the most familiar requests in the teaching of Meditation. It sounds so simple and right, yet we find it very difficult to carry out. If only we can practise trusting in God so completely in our times of silence that the divine power within our sentence can show us what is right, then we become more able to think, feel, and act, according to that Power, which will grow in us until it becomes an unconscious aid to more righteous living.

We cannot help but organise our lives within the structures set up by present day society. Yet we dare not lose sight of the higher spiritual values which give true security and protection from the world's standards.

We cannot put our trust completely in money, in position or in any organisation that man has set up, for, if they are taken away what then can support us? "Trust thou only in Me" we are asked.

Until we find that true foundation for living we exist as on a quicksand with doubt and even fear in our step; but when we turn within and reach that point where life should be lived out, the Spirit will lead us in the paths of righteousness where all things are in His keeping.

This does not necessarily mean that we opt out of our responsibilities but it does mean that we look first to God, and in so doing we become stronger than the world's power over us.

Nor does God deny us the good things of this world. On the contrary He gives them to us in full measure as we learn to trust in Him and use these things aright.

"Trust thou only in Me and I will give thee the power of Righteousness."

Pause for silent meditation.

"I will give thee the Power of Righteousness".

These words may well pull us up short when we begin to use them in meditation, but surely this is a helpful sign for it prevents us from slipping into the half conscious repetition of the more familiar form of sentence.

When we come up against something unfamiliar, it maybe a new gadget of some kind, we don't just accept it at face value, we want to examine the goods ourselves before we accept them.

It is just the same with our sentence. We are not expected to use the words without first getting the feel of them in our minds. Then they can be put to work for us in our times of silence.

Yet our sentence is only the vessel within which spiritual truth is contained, and when that truth is accepted and becomes active within us, our vessel is no longer necessary. Therefore we use our sentence with care and precision, so that all that it contains is released within us and we rest in the freeing, healing power of righteousness.

Can we imagine what it would be like to stand completely free of all inner conflict, of physical weariness or frustration—to feel only that deep inner security which springs from practising the presence of God within?

Let this time of silence be an opportunity to practise trusting completely in the Power of Righteousness. For, in the stillness of mind and body, we can more easily lay down our doubts, our fears, our frustrations before our Lord and give our whole attention to Him.

For instance, we might relax that grim determination to put things right with so and so; or pause before writing that letter which might state our case but could also injure someone else's feelings. Recognise and turn away from any hint of self righteous thinking or feeling. Leave all this and

29

more at the door of our Lord's temple before we enter in for we are His temple and He waits at the altar of our souls.

Only when we are right with God can His Power be entrusted to us, and when we reach true stillness within, there also lies true security and power which does not depend on any outer conditions but upon God alone.

"Trust thou only in Me and I will give thee the Power of Righteousness".

Pause for silent meditation.

Perhaps it is because our ideas of power are so worldly that we find it a bit disconcerting when it is linked with righteousness. We tend to think of power in terms of strength, driving force or energy. These are only the results of power which have already been harnessed. We cannot see power at its source, where it is untapped. Take electricity for example – we cannot see it in its potential state yet it is all around us, it is part of our physical being. It is the use we put it to that makes power visible.

We cannot see the power of God within us. Yet it is through His righteousness being expressed to some degree in our lives that tells us of His presence, and when we catch a glimpse of the righteousness of God in stillness we are given a clearer view of our own misplaced actions and how best to redirect our energies.

We are often prevented from finding the Kingdom of Righteousness by the very fact that we are not quite prepared to accept its standards. If we truly seek righteousness within we need to be able to face the things which are not quite right in ourselves. The righteousness can have no power over our circumstances if we are content to compromise or look for the best of both worlds; e.g. we may have turned our backs upon an opportunity which truly could have fulfilled our lives, but, because our trust in divine help was not quite strong enough and another tempting desire of a more worldly nature came along, we chose to leave the higher work unattended. At this point we try to convince ourselves that we are just not fitted for higher work and eventually we begin to believe it.

We tell ourselves comfortingly that that would just not have been me. Of course it wouldn't be us – not as we are now – but it could be us as God wants us to be if we trusted in the power of His righteousness to add all things unto us.

Let us take that one step further in faith by the use of this sentence now.

"Trust thou only in Me and I will give thee the power of Righteousness."

Pause for silent meditation.

"I am Infinite Peace within thee. With My Peace I give thee rest."

The quality of rest which we achieve through practising stillness in the presence of Christ brings with it true peace of mind, ease of body and contentment to the soul. This kind of rest is far from a condition of idleness. It is a state of harmony and completeness when all our energies are directed towards the centre of divine life within us and gently focussed there. Then the giver of that life holds us, guides and prepares us for His service. This focussing of our attention can be likened to looking through a magnifying glass, to concentrate our visual energies upon a particular object to enhance its detail.

When we look within we use our sentence in a similar way, to focus our inner eyes without distraction upon the infinite peace of God, to increase our awareness of Him. Also when we rest calmly in the words of this meditation we are free from doubt and fear, even if only for a space. For our Lord said, "Let not your heart be troubled, neither let it be afraid. My Peace I give unto you."

Yet we continue to let our disturbing memories weigh us down and allow our vivid imagination to fill us with apprehension for the future. The birds and animals do not concern themselves, either with the past or with the future; they simply accept life as it is now and live it moment by moment, for they have no choice. We as human beings have been endowed with very fertile minds which function in many directions, but we have also been given the will and the awareness to help us bring our whole consciousness under the loving care of the Spirit within us.

In this way we find freedom from our past. We use our memories in a positive creative way by willingly accepting

the responsibilities for our mistakes, turning them into wel-
come opportunities for new and vital experiences for the
future.

We can also use our lively imaginations to help visualise
and hold to the truth of the Spirit within us before we enter
stillness, and when we come to our time of silence know,
that in ever increasing power, that Spirit will set us free
from all that falls short of His truth in our past as we truly
rest in His peace.

"Come unto me all ye that labour and are heavy laden
and I will give thee rest." Matt. 11:28.

Let the whole mind be filled with the truth of this meditation till we know nothing else, then troubles are banished by
the peace of Christ indwelling us.

"I am Infinite Peace within thee. With My Peace I give
thee rest."

Pause for silent meditation.

The practice of contemplative meditation can lead us to a
deeper and more intimate relationship with Christ, which He
offers us when He says "Take my yoke upon you and learn
of Me, for My yoke is easy and my burden is light." Matt.
11:29-30.

When we turn to our Lord in stillness, and there rest easy
in His presence with the idea of being inwardly yoked to
Him, sharing His Life, we learn of Him. This helps us take
one step further to let go our own restless self-seeking, leaving room, in our hearts and minds, for the infinite peace of
God to take its place.

To be inwardly yoked with Christ means that we no
longer back away from Him in case too much might be
asked of us. Later, when our thought and feeling nature
begins to respond consciously to the divine influence of
Christ, the unconscious mind within, where many of our
conflicts arise, also begins to accept this new direction for

living. Then we are much less likely to be the victims of our own human impulses, and much more at peace within ourselves.

There is no outward comparison which can adequately express the inner spiritual relationship which develops when we stay inwardly yoked with Christ. Yet, perhaps the physical partnership which exists between a blind person and their guide dog can emphasise a need for both a method of training and dedication to practise, before any real partnership can grow.

When the dog and its owner begin to work together they act individually, according to the rules, but as they get used to being harnessed together, a bond of affection is formed between them. By this time the discipline of training and practice is being translated into a mutual acceptance of love and sharing. The dog and owner are becoming one unit of consciousness, and what had been achieved strenuously by individual attention to method now becomes a happy joint activity of freedom. What was once a form of practice now becomes an unconscious unity of movement and co-ordination.

If such can be the partnership between an animal and a human being, exercised at the level of physical mobility, how perfectly complete is the unity in the Spirit which we can enjoy when we turn to the divine master within and slip into that easy yoke which He holds for us.

Our method and practice of meditation will soon be translated into a more personal relationship with Christ and a knowledge of His infinite peace in our hearts.

Let us take up our sentence now and by the gentle repetition of the words, slip into that easy yoke that waits for us. Here we rest, assured that all our problems are being shared and the strength to meet them is also given.

"I am Infinite Peace within thee. With My Peace I give thee rest."

Pause for silent meditation.

This meditation helps us to realise that we are being offered by our Lord Himself, much more than we can ever imagine. We are being offered that peace which the world cannot give – Infinite Peace – which is beyond our understanding.

When we try to understand something by ourselves it usually means that we analyse and then arrive at some conclusion. At least for the moment we feel satisfied but this is only the beginning as far as contemplative meditation is concerned. We do, of course, need to accept intellectually the validity and power of the divine truth, which we hold in stillness, but, from that point on we learn to trust to the Holy Spirit behind our meditation to enlighten us. For the intellect takes a rest in our times of meditation. Although our sentence tells us much it reveals little of its true spiritual content until we take it beyond the mental barriers of our own incomprehension. Then the Spirit of peace can lead us straight to the vital centre of our being where infinite life is set free.

That which in our sentence lies beyond our understanding we accept in faith, knowing that when we enter stillness, leaving our own ideas behind, what we receive of the Spirit is beyond words.

Each time of silence is a new and enriching experience, whether we realise it or not, for the inner working of the Spirit will be manifest in His time and according to our deepest need.

May we prepare to receive something of that true peace of mind, ease of body, and contentment of the soul, which the world cannot give.

"I am Infinite Peace within thee. With My Peace I give thee rest."

Pause for silent meditation.

I am Infinite Love within thee. I will give thee the hidden riches of secret places.''

When we are first introduced to this way of meditation, the method used may seem to be a little artificial. The repetition of a sentence does not appeal to our imagination or fit in with our ideas of spiritual teaching.

Yet with further inspection we find that the sentences chosen contain much more than words. As we repeat a sentence within ourselves, becoming one with its rhythm and its truth, we find that we are not lulled into passive acquiescence, as we might be when soothed by persuasive suggestions. No, our hearts and minds are being alerted by the hidden power within our sentence, for the words which we repeat are of a divine creative order, capable of awakening the Spirit of Infinite Love within us as they are fed into our inner being. For words have both an outer and an inner meaning. They say something to the conscious mind and later they reveal something to the soul.

Meditation offers in condensed form the essence of divine teaching in the shape of a sentence and when the outer meaning is acceptable to us the words are quietly dropped into the unconscious nature, like seeds being planted in the dark soil of our being, where in time, the spiritual riches within the words are brought forth by the Spirit of Infinite Love Himself to enrich our lives.

Just as the plant seeds in the earth seek out the source of growth within the dark soil before they push upwards towards the transforming light of the sun, so too do the seeds of infinite love planted in our consciousness seek out the hidden source of spiritual growth, before they can show forth as new enlightenment and understanding in our lives.

"I will give thee the treasures of darkness and hidden riches of secret places." Isaiah 45:3. These words from the

Old Testament show us that the Bible too has both an outer and an inner meaning. It can be accepted simply as historical or eternal fact, but the inner meaning has to be felt in the heart.

When Jesus spoke to His followers, he often used words and teaching which they could not then fully understand, but as they came to know Jesus, they learned to accept His words in faith, and understanding came later.

In the New Testament the parable of the sower scattering his seed on both the fertile and infertile soil alike is a good example of Jesus's teaching. The outer meaning of this story is quite obvious, but the inner meaning which Jesus had to explain to His listeners, has to be sought. Jesus said "He that hath ears to hear, let him hear.". Luke 8:8.

The seed is the word of God and to you it is given to know the mysteries of the Kingdom of God.

Let us use our sentence now with increased anticipation of the power of infinite love to enrich our lives, till something of the hidden riches can be found.

"I am Infinite Love within thee. I will give thee the hidden riches of secret places."

Pause for silent meditation.

This particular sentence holds a real attraction for us because of the sense of mystery it awakens: that same divine mystery which surrounds the whole Christian faith, which only Christ can unfold within each receptive soul as we appeal to Him.

Many of our meditations begin with the statement, "I Am." as spoken by God Himself. This is one of the most profound and mysterious names which God gives to Himself. "I Am, that I Am." Exod. 3:14.

We feel it very difficult to relate to the "I Am" within us, yet when we recognise Him in the divine nature of Christ, who demonstrated the infinite love of God throughout His earthly life, the words of our meditation can become alive and meaningful for us. For, our Lord also said it of Himself,

"Before Abraham was I am." John 8:58. Perhaps from these words we can realise at least something of the underlying feeling of infinity, which this meditation should convey to us and gain a real sense of the everlasting nature of God's love, which was in the beginning is now and ever shall be.

In Genesis we read "In the beginning God created the heavens and the earth... and man in His own image." Gen. 1:1-27. God created the heavens and the earth, that is, the inner and the outer worlds and man in His own image, which is the inner creative Spirit and the outer visible being. All God's creation has both an inner and an outer aspect, and what God creates He inhabits and sustains. God's love within us endures all things even our lack of response to Himself. He suffers with infinite patience.

Let infinite love speak within us now, filling our human consciousness with a truer realisation of the infinite love of God, who is eternally giving, sharing His life with us. For our Lord said, "It is your Father's good pleasure to give you the kingdom." Luke 12:32.

"I am Infinite Love within thee. I will give thee the hidden riches of secret places."

Pause for silent meditation.

Meditation helps us to find the spiritual riches which often lie hidden just because we have become so used to our spiritual poverty that we look for nothing more. Should we value too highly the world's riches, neglecting to seek the undiscovered spiritual treasures within, we are like that tiny seed which turns all its energies towards the warmth and brilliance of the sun, without first establishing its inner strength and security within the earth.

As we approach the next silence we become more aware of the two aspects of our own being, the visible and the invisible, and when we draw our outer strength from that which is within we become one with the "I Am", who longs to live in us.

Our Lord Himself said that when we pray, we should

retire into our own room by ourselves, to be with the Father. In the prayer of contemplation we do just that. We practise the prayer of listening. We enter into the secret place of the most high within, the temple of our own body, for there the Spirit of Infinite Love is free to enlighten us without the outside world distracting our attention from Him.

The repetition of our sentence cannot by itself heal us of all that comes between us and the Spirit of Infinite Love. It is when we come in true humility to be freed from our secret faults, when the thinking mind is shut off in stillness, that our sentence can lead us from the visible world of the senses to the invisible world of the spirit. Then we need no longer fear the dark or unknown way, for infinite love will be our guide and the "I Am" within us draws us to Himself.

Let us enter the secret place of the most high within and find the treasures of the world fade into insignificance, as the spiritual riches of the inner life become more real to us.

"I am Infinite Love within thee. I will give thee the hidden riches of secret places."

Pause for silent meditation.

"Eternal Love within me. Thee only will I serve."

We often find ourselves coming to a cross-roads in life with problems to solve and decisions to make, yet even before we have begun to see what is expected of us, we start to worry. We actually exhaust ourselves by trying to weigh up all the many possibilities that might arise and so waste precious energy which should have been used in carrying out the real tasks when they came along.

Why do we worry and become so over-concerned about our future? Is it that we just do not know God well enough and cannot have sufficient faith in His eternal love?

It is easy to become so devastated by human problems that we are quite incapable of seeing the love of God within whatever we are trying to carry out in our own strength. This can lead to a feeling of real hopelessness, of separation from God, which we have to admit to at times, for we so often shut God out of our lives and leave little time to be with Him. Yet it is the same feeling of separateness from God which the regular practice of meditation can help us to overcome, if we will let it.

If we quietly and patiently learn to be still in mind and body for a little while each day, (even though our surroundings are far from helpful,) when we truly seek to know God and His love for us, we shall find a time and a place to be with Him. Then when we are 'one pointed' in thought and desire, God will take charge of our silence so that His love may be made known to us.

Thus, we come to each time of silence, no longer full of our own ideas, expecting God to give His approval, but putting our own solutions aside, no matter how precious to us, and let God come into the centre of our meditation. Only then can our growing love for Him make His love more plain to us.

Then surely do we begin to live with confidence and hope, when we find that even some of our own ideas have received the blessing of our Lord.

So we approach Him now in this silence, knowing that by our coming, we serve Him in part, so that later He may enable us to serve Him more perfectly.

"Eternal Love within me. Thee only will I serve."

Pause for silent meditation.

Many of our ways of thinking and feeling have been conditioned by the thoughts and feelings of past generations, for we inherit a mixture of the weaknesses and failings which our ancestors have accumulated for us, as well as the highest and best which we, as the human race, have yet reached.

It is this highest and best which must be brought forth from within us and the weaknesses and failings strengthened or eliminated from our nature.

This is what takes place during our times of silence, no matter what sentence we are using, for each sentence enfolds a word of life, which is one aspect of the divine nature of God. As we quietly absorb each of these qualities into our minds and thence into our souls, our transformation is both gentle and balanced.

As we continue in the practice of Contemplative Meditation over the weeks, we begin to recognise some of the changes which have been taking place in us. For instance, many of the little faults in our behaviour towards others, which we were quite happy to ignore in the past, now disturb us. They keep nagging at our conscience though we quite conscientiously try to eliminate them from our personality. For we are beginning to understand that this way of meditation is a way of life and as we faithfully practise through the months we begin to live by its teaching. We find we are more able to reach stillness, to hold each of the words of life for a time, letting them help in the gradual transformation of all that is contrary to them in our nature, till such qualities as eternal love, infinite joy, or divine wisdom can become our own. Sometimes, in a very natural way, we are apt to confine these divine qualities within us to a very human manner of expression. We think in terms of human joys, physical beauty, worldly wisdom, confining our own development to a very worldly level.

Take human love for example. How often do we stunt its growth or taint its beauty with feelings of possessiveness, selfishness or just pettedness, instead of upholding that love in our heart before God so that He might transform it, in the silence of our meditation, into a truly spiritual energy, full of His power. Then God could direct that energy as a rich self-sacrificing joyful force released into His world.

Let us find that kind of love now in the silence of our meditation.

"Eternal love within me. Thee only will I serve."

Pause for silent meditation.

The eternal love of God is experienced by us from within, for that is where our direct contact with God is to be made. God can reveal Himself to us in things, through people and all nature's activity around us, but we have to go within to make our own personal contact with Him.

Our Lord himself said "Neither shall they say lo here or lo there, for behold, the kingdom of God is within you." Luke 17:21.

God enlightens us from within when we have no outward distractions to divert our attention from Him. When we meditate upon the love of God we are in tune with Him and learn to grow in His likeness.

The idea that divine love already lies within us or that God teaches us from within, may be new to us. But, when we look at one of the very simplest and most natural examples of indwelling life in the physical form and we realise that the same law applies spiritually, we may have much less difficulty in accepting this truth. Look at the apples on a tree when they are beginning to ripen. Where does their life come from? Not from outside themselves, although the sunshine and rain, helps them to grow outwardly. No, their life comes from within, from their contact with the central life of the apple tree. But, should we unthinkingly damage a branch of the tree, the fruit at the end of that branch may not be able to draw fully of that life giving sap of the tree and so cannot ripen to full perfection.

Similarly it can be for ourselves. If we carelessly allow the channel of divine life and love within us to become blocked, by our concern, hurt feelings or any other devitalising tendency, then we too can only live according to the quality of life which we are able to receive.

When we draw divine life and love direct from its true source, ever waiting within us, our lives will be constantly renewed and enriched. The Spirit will no longer be hindered by our wrong ways of thinking and feeling, for divine love brings harmony and healing in their place, helping us towards full spiritual maturity.

"Eternal Love within me. Thee only will I serve."

Pause for silent meditation.

"O God, give me Knowledge, Knowledge of Thy Health and healing Power within me."

This sentence may seem a bit daunting to begin with, because Knowledge is not easy to accept as a Word of Life. Our ideas of knowledge are of something to be acquired by study, or received through the senses or emotional experiences, but in this meditation we are asking for Knowledge from a higher source, from the very fountain of all knowledge, the Christ within. (Col. 2: 2-3.) In order to receive it we must still our minds, and wait patiently for the little flashes of enlightenment which not only increase our understanding of deep spiritual truths, but direct our natural powers and intellectual gifts, real or potential, into more creative channels.

This experience will help us to see that if we rely on knowledge which is based solely on our human activities of thought, feeling and experience, personal or inherited, our lives will be shaped according to these set patterns, leaving little room for the expansion of a higher consciousness. St. Paul tells us: "Adapt yourselves no longer to the pattern of this present world, but let your minds be remade and your whole nature thus transformed" Romans 12:2. New English Bible.

As we rest our whole attention upon the indwelling Spirit of Christ our consciousness is quickened, for His Divine Knowledge, as we receive it, is both living and creative, given for the purpose of sharing its fruits at all levels of living.

Let us now prepare ourselves to receive this gift of divine Knowledge. As it filters through our over-burdened consciousness in the stillness of meditation, the human knowledge already stored in our minds will be clarified and enlightened and put to the highest use, for Our Lord said:

"Behold, I make all things new." Revelations 21:5

O God, give me Knowledge, Knowledge of Thy Health and healing Power within me.

Pause for silent meditation

Health is a condition which we usually think of as confined to physical fitness and well-being, yet we are beginning to realise just how much our physical health is affected by our mental and emotional states. The various aspects of our being, which make up the whole, cannot be divided into watertight compartments. The physical, mental and emotional states interact, making us the kind of person we are. Yet we must always bear in mind that within us is an even deeper area, the collective unconscious of humanity, from which many of our actions and instinctive reactions arise; therefore our characters are not only an expression of personal thoughts, feelings and experiences, but also reflect patterns inherited from past generations, or absorbed from our environment. It is from the deep collective unconscious mind that many obscure causes of sickness or physical disorder arise, but when we open our hearts to the Spirit, the Light of Divine Knowledge will shine through our inner darkness, dispersing the shadows of ignorance and fear, and then true healing begins in the depth of our being.

There are many strange, varied and psychosomatic causes of disease. Even an undefined fear can play havoc with our health. Fear of inadequacy can make some people find a morbid satisfaction in being ill; it may be an unconscious shield protecting them from responsibilities which are too great for them to bear. When Jesus healed the sick, He had the Power to see each person against the background of humanity. He understood the inheritance from the collective unconscious which affected each soul. He dealt with each person individually. He knew their personal weaknesses, the doubts, fears and ignorance which were restricting their spiritual growth. Jesus did not seek out people to heal their diseases, but to awaken their faith in God's Infinite Love.

As his hearers listened to His words and accepted the truth in their hearts, healing was the natural result. "According to your faith be it unto you" (Matthew 9:29). Those who felt His great compassion and witnessed His powers, recognised Him as the Divine Physician, and sought His help with quickened faith.

Let us once again listen to the words of our meditation— hear them just as though Our Lord were speaking them within our own souls, and turn to the divine Physician and Master, leaving all else to Him.

O God, give me Knowledge, Knowledge of Thy Health and healing Power within me.

Pause for silent meditation

We can keep a wound clean and protect it from outside infection, but it is the natural healing power within us which repairs the damage. We can help to replace our injured feelings with understanding forgiveness, and lift our wayward minds above damaging thoughts and ideas, but only as we seek Knowledge of God and His indwelling Spirit can He do His healing work within our souls.

Just as we do not know the true origin of our ills, neither are we capable of knowing the degree or nature of the inner healing which is taking place during our times of silence. Yet we can sometimes recognise some of the results; for where there is a growing Knowledge of God in our hearts there is also a lessening of tension in our lives. This leads to an increase in physical well-being, and our strength is sufficient for all our needs.

People sometimes torment themselves by attempting to dig up buried memories which might be the cause of present ills, but this distressing process need not be suffered when we approach the Divine Physician in stillness. For our growing trust in Him, and His Knowledge of all that we are, can free us from all our unnecessary burdens, and only those things which can further our spiritual growth will be brought to our attention. As we view these particular memories in

46

the Light and Knowledge of God's Love, hidden fears are melted away and cease to have any power over us. Our problems are healed not only in their results, but at their source.

When we think of the healing miracles of Jesus it all seems very far from the present day. Yet that is not so, according to His teaching. What Jesus gave to the world He did not take away when He left it. During His earthly life Our Lord could reach only those people with whom He came into contact at that time, but His promise was that when He ascended to the Father He would send the Holy Spirit, who would not be confined to one human body, or to time and space, but would live within the hearts of those who would turn to Him. This Knowledge has not only to be accepted in our hearts and minds, but turned into experience in our lives; for the Divine Physician and Master lives and works just as much today as He did in the past for those who listen to His words. Seek Him out for healing, and hear Him say: "Thy faith hath made thee whole." Mark 5:34.

O God, give me Knowledge. Knowledge of Thy Health and healing Power within me.

Pause for silent meditation

"I am eternal Life within thee. Behold, I make all things new".

We are apt to look upon eternal life as something belonging only to the future; a form of existence quite out of our reach here and now, but when we take time to dwell upon the idea of eternal life being always with us, we realise that it must be behind our whole human existence. God gives Himself to us in such a way that each human being represents His eternal spirit being individualised, giving to each and all the freedom to express His Spirit in countless ways. Yet the spirit of God can never be diminished by such bountiful giving, for each individualised spark of the eternal Spirit remains as pure as the source from which it springs, in God the Father. It is our neglect of this precious gift of God and our human need to feel self assertive and independent that has weakened the spiritual resources of humanity to such a degree that we often lose the sense of belonging to God and our human desire for Him.

Jesus likened the spirit of eternal life within us to a well of living water springing up into eternal life, by which, when we find it, our thirst for fulfilment will be quenched. When we open our hearts and minds to the purifying springs of living water within us, we find in time that all our doubts and fears and the debris of worn out thoughts and feelings that we have allowed to gather there will be replaced by the light of the eternal life itself. Then indeed all things are surely being made new by a new reverence for life itself, a growing realisation of the oneness of all life in God the Father, and a new joy and inner security that this awareness brings.

Let us hear the words of our meditation now in this silence:-

"I am Eternal Life within thee. Behold, I make all things new."

Pause for silent meditation.

In the book of Job, Chapter 33, Verse 4, in spite of much suffering and inner turmoil Job was able to say–"The spirit of God hath made me and the breath of the Almighty giveth me life."

Meditation helps us, not only to believe this truth in our hearts and minds, but to become more and more aware of the eternal presence within our whole being. God the Father is the creator of the whole universe and what God creates He inhabits and sustains till His purpose is complete. God created man in His own image, therefore each living soul has that spirit of God behind the life within him.

In human terms when we try to create something, be it baking a cake, writing a letter, or even painting a picture, there is always something of our own human nature being expressed in what we produce. Yet that creative impulse can be purified and increased in us when we become alive to our eternal inheritance.

Christ came to earth to awaken that God spirit within us, and as we become more attentive to Christ's words and listen to them in our hearts, the spirit of God is quickened and we become more sensitive to Christ's teaching. We remind ourselves that there is something of God's spirit in what He speaks, for when Christ speaks a word, or makes a promise, that word, that promise is already fulfilled, waiting only to be accepted by us. What we have to do is to be ready to receive. Meditation should become a two way communion with Christ. We approach Him in silence and wait upon Him in stillness, till His creative Life can be expressed in our lives.

We may sometimes hear it said that our Lord never taught meditation, yet we read many times in the scriptures, how He departed up into a mountain or to a quiet place, to be alone with God the Father. The word meditation may not have been used but Christ being the son of God, did not need to learn how to commune with God. He was one with God and by going apart from others found His meditative state by which He absorbed without distraction all that God, the father, had to impart to Him.

If Christ felt the need to withdraw from people, to be alone with God, how much more do we need to learn the importance of finding a way of coming into closer communion with the most High, so that we might learn of Him.

May the power of the living word, the creative activity of the spirit, help us to enjoy the more abundant life which Christ came to share.

"I am Eternal Life within thee. Behold, I make all things new."

Pause for silent meditation.

"Behold, I make all things new."

To behold, does not simply mean to look at and see with the outward eye. When Jesus used the word He was asking people to pay attention to discern inwardly what lay behind the obvious situation.

"Behold, I make all things new."

The changes we refer to here cannot be observed outwardly until they have first taken place within us by the gentle transmutation of all that is out of tune with the spirit of Christ.

Have we learned nothing from the experience of the disciples? Surely there was ample reason for their reticence in accepting such radical teaching as Jesus gave. They could not accept all that he taught them. It was all so different from the old mistaken beliefs that they knew. But we, surely, should have gained some understanding of Jesus's teaching from the changes which took place in the disciples themselves, after the resurrection of Christ when the Holy Spirit came to them and renewed their lives. Many enlightened souls who have since beheld the true light of the spirit throughout the centuries that followed have given us priceless proof of the continuing activity of the Holy Spirit ceaselessly seeking to increase our spiritual awareness and purpose for living.

Yet surely the area in which we gain most hope from the disciples lives is from their very human weaknesses. We can identify with their doubts and fears and their disloyalty. We can stand with them knowing that in their plight we too can take courage and still have faith, knowing that all things are indeed being made new in a way that brings us towards closer communion with God through Christ our Lord.

Let us take our sentence now in faith:-

"I am Eternal Life within thee. Behold, I make all things new."

Pause for silent meditation.

My servant art thou, in whom I shall break into glory."

This sentence may at first seem a little out of our grasp. We feel slightly presumptuous when we try to apply it to ourselves. Yet it is God's glory which is being offered us, and it is our Lord who is actually calling us His servants—people of whom He might be able to say "I call you friends".

In many ways the true image of service has become tarnished or lost and many types of modern employment do little to make us feel that the work that we do can really help satisfy the needs of others. What we are most conscious of is the boredom of monotonous tasks done with little sense of purpose. Yet this is very far from the attitude which Jesus held towards work or service of any kind.

From the human angle our view of life is very limited, but as we affirm that it is Christ our Divine Master whom we would serve, our whole attitude towards life's conditions undergoes a change. This does not necessarily mean that we are being asked to drop our present way of living, as the disciples did in Jesus's time, but it does mean that no matter our work, or even pleasures, these activities should be carried out as in the presence of our Loving Master.

We can never find real satisfaction in our work until we see Christ at the centre of life. Then, when we turn to His indwelling spirit, He will point out the imperfections of our vision and help us see service in the Light of God's glory and love.

As we get to know and love our Divine Master day by day, we come to the realisation that there are two ways of serving. The first and highest is unseen, passive, inward toward the Spirit in stillness. The second, arising directly from the first, is visible, practical, outward towards others,

When we begin to live by these two ways of serving, we develop a deeper sensitivity to the needs of others. We no longer offer the kind of help that we think is necessary, instead we wait to be shown the deeper need. This is the beginning of the true servant and master relationship which leads to an ever deepening experience of the glory and love of Christ, seeking expression within our own lives. Then even the dullest task, done for Christ's sake, sheds a tiny gleam of the glory and love of God into the darker side of life.

"My servant art thou, in whom I shall break into Glory."

Pause for silent meditation.

As with service, glory also has lost much of its pure meaning in our minds, and is more often used in a frivolous way in daily conversation. Yet we need only turn our attention to the outward expression of God's glory in the natural world, and learn much from its response to God's power at work, within its varying forms.

We see how each realm of nature shows forth the glory of God with an unconscious, unswerving devotion, fulfilling its evolving plan with robust vigour. There is no enmity in nature; she simply follows the many patterns of life to be unfolded, accepting and adapting to the changing elements in her present environment, bringing glory even to the most unexpected places.

Yet we who have been given awareness and choice, fall far short of expressing God's glory and love because of our very human urge to be self- assertive and independent. We tend to fight against unhappy conditions, and even resent them, and we sometimes fail to co-operate with changing circumstances instead of accepting the challenge of inner growth and enlightenment, which these opportunities give us.

Should we seek happiness only through worldly goods and human joys, forgetful of the higher spiritual values, our materialistic attitude may not only confine us to a very human level of expression, it can limit God's gifts to us accordingly. For we have turned towards the glorification of the personal self which shuts out the true glory, which can enrich our lives.

When we recognise that deep within each one of us is a growing longing of the soul towards God, which only God can satisfy, we see the futility of trying to build our own little strongholds of worldly security, but rely upon the indwelling love of God to sustain and protect us.

We need to create within our own hearts and minds, the right environment wherein the light of Divine Glory and Love can be set free, bringing real strength and stability into our lives.

As we gently hold the words of our meditation during this silence our whole being is made ready to receive that particular aspect of Divine Glory and Love which it is our part to express in the world.

"My servant art thou, in whom I shall break into Glory."

Pause for silent meditation.

True Christian service can be undertaken more happily and completely if we understand and exercise a certain amount of detachment. This at first may strike a chilly note of uncaring in our minds, but this should not be so. For how could our student doctors and nurses ever learn to practise their profession or how could our mine, air and sea rescue teams do their work of mercy, if they allowed every victim in distress to reduce them to a state of emotional immobility?

Yet compassion is as important as detachment; together they give strength, Compassion enables us to identify with the sufferer, detachment protects us from the power of the negative conditions in which the sufferer is placed. Both spring from the infinite love and compassion of Christ Himself.

Just as the disciples called upon the Master in their distress at sea, so we call upon the Divine Master within to do His work of rescue through us. It is only by using some degree of detachment that we can make that inner call by a

Word of Life, coming either voluntarily or involuntarily to our aid. This opens that inner door to the Spirit of Love and compassion. Then the answering flow of Divine Life which we seek, can reach out and awaken something of that same feeling in the one we wish to help. There seems no better way of serving than to help others become more aware of the glory and love of God, seeking expression within their own lives.

May we seek to serve in this silence, letting the words come alive for us, and thereafter, work through us.

"My servant art thou, in whom I shall break into Glory."

Pause for silent meditation.

Thanksgiving

It is not enough to read or talk about meditation. It is when we take time to practise and experience its results in our daily lives that we open our hearts and give thanks – saying...

"Bless the Lord, oh my soul, and all that is within me, bless His Holy Name." Psalm 103: 1.

Isabel Henderson.

Words of Life
BE still and know that I AM
GOD
Spirit
Life
Knowledge
Power
Holiness
Faith
Health
Wealth
Unity
Love
Joy
Peace
Righteousness
Wisdom
Goodness
Grace
Truth
Beauty
Freedom
Principle

I AM thy Holy and Eternal Substance, Omniscient, Omnipotent, Omnipresent, and there is none beside ME

Index of Biblical Quotations

A sower went out to sow   Luke 8:5-15
The Kingdom of God is within you   Luke 17:21
Know ye not that ye are the temple of God   1 Cor. 3:16
Behold, I have loved thee   Jer. 31:3
Peace, be still   Mark 4:39
I am the way, the Truth & the Life   John 14:6
He that followeth me   John 8:12
I will give thee the treasures of darkness   Isaiah 45:3
Let not your heart be troubled   John 14:27
Come unto me   Matt. 11:28
Take my yoke upon you   Matt. 11:29-30
He that hath ears to hear, let him hear   Luke 8:8
I am, that I am   Exod. 3:14
Before Abraham was I am   John 8:58
In the beginning God created   Gen. 1:1-27
It is your Father's good pleasure   Luke 12:32
Neither shall they say lo here   Luke 17:21
Behold, I make all things new   Rev. 21:5
According to your faith   Matt. 9:29
Thy faith hath made thee whole   Mark 5:34
Bless the Lord, oh my soul   Psalm 103:1